From Wandering To Wonderful- Navigating To Life's Sweet Spot

Table of Contents

Book Description

If you are anything like me, you have a desired life in mind. As a human being, it is in your nature to want to find happiness in life. In order to live that life, there are certain things that will help and hinder you. It is important to understand what those things are so you can start a journey to live your life completely and happily.

This booklet will help you do that with 52 steps guaranteed to set you off in the right direction. In order to live the life you are meant to live, you must stop doing the things that are hindering you, as well as developing some habits that will move you forward. It is difficult to just wake up and start living life with purpose. This book will give you steps to set you on your path "From Wandering to Wonderful".

Smooches!

Jennise Beverly

Acknowledgement

I would like to send a heartfelt "thank you" out to everyone that I have met along my journey that changed me in such a way that made me realize I needed to move from Wandering to Wonderful.

My mom Georgia Beverly, thank you for believing I could even when I had no idea if I would or not. You have been my sounding board for many nights and I love and appreciate you for that. I would not have written this book if you had not pumped me up to believe I could.

My dad for the insights to living my life, based on my terms and conditions. You have affected me in more ways than you will ever know. I love you, man.

My sister for your grace and for how you bounced back from breast cancer and started living your life on purpose, for this I love and cherish you.

My children Jordyn and Zaria. You're the reason I was able to go on after the storm, the reason I get up and hit that sweet spot every day. You are my air, my why, the true loves of my life.

My girls, Dommonique, Tricia, Michelle, Robin, Reba, Joann, Lisa, Tonya and Keshia. What can I say, I was able to bounce back and start living because I had each of you along the way to help me reinvent myself, and to appreciate and start living. Each of you has helped me do just that. I love you all to the moon and back a trillion times.

My brother from another mother Bryan Spearman. You came into my life after the storm and made me realize just what I was missing: a brother. You have encouraged me and believed in me in ways only a brother could. Thanks for loving and accepting me just as I am. I hear your voice saying all the time, you're the bomb. I appreciate and love you.

Last, but certainly not least. Henry Gentry, you came into my life and taught me balance and gave me more than a million reasons to smile, and to know that life is sweet. I love you and appreciate the voice of reason and balance that you brought to my life.

Introduction: Living and Learning

I am passionate about many things, and not so passionate about many others. I believe in order to live life to the fullest; there are key things that one must adhere to such as proper diet, exercise, and worship. Outside of these key things, I feel life should be lived authentically, and this can mean something very different for each person.

Now, for me this was not always the case. There was a time in my life when living inside of the box was the only life I knew, and I embraced the safety and predictability. After many decades of living the safe predictable life, a storm blew in my life that would forever change me. This storm would force me to live my life authentically. In the midst of a storm, one of two things will happen. We will fold and succumb to the trial, or we will fight to survive and recover.

In 2009 a major life storm blew in and stripped me away from the comfortable box I had lived in for over 3 decades. Lost, exposed and hopeless I begin to search high and low for another box to live in. With no such luck, life made me desperate in search for a new start. This began my journey from "Wandering to Wonderful" in search of my "Sweet Spot".

In searching for my "Sweet Spot" I realized I had not been living the best life fit for me. In the several years after the storm I would search within and write the things I needed to stop doing to start living a life outside the box, outside the walls that either I built or allowed others to build in around me. In addition to the things I needed to stop doing, I felt it was essential for me to find the things I needed to start doing to make sure I was living my best life. This would lead to years of shedding old layers to allow the most authentic and freshest parts of who I was to shine through.

If you feel like you are not living your absolute best life, this book will open your mind and eyes to some great possibilities. Read on and experience the changes for yourself. The whole world is opening up to you, enjoy the view.

52 Steps To Your "Sweet Spot"

STEP 1

Stop spending time and energy on people or activities that you don't enjoy

The opportunities for enjoyment in your life are limitless. If you are not experiencing enough joy, you have only yourself to blame.

– David E. Bresler

In 2009, the phrase "Life is too short" took on an entirely new meaning. My fiancée died in a car accident at the age of 30. Life as I knew it changed drastically. My love, my life, and my future with him were instantly over. I had to learn how to face the coming days. It was this life challenge that would open my eyes to an entire different perspective.

Things I used to fret over no longer mattered. I would hear my girlfriends and other people around me complaining about their relationships, jobs, or family and I would think to myself, is this person really serious? Surely they are not fretting over this. As I would sit and listen to their complaints, one question echoed in my mind. If you knew you were going to die tomorrow, how relevant would this be?

Over the course of my stages of grief, I begin to replay conversations that I had with my love shortly before he died over in over in my head. Three days before he died we had a conversation about work, and I was complaining. He looked at me and said, "Promise me you will start looking for another job after the baby is born no matter what happens. Why stay there if you're miserable?"

Several days later, he would be gone and I would be left to ponder that conversation until my mind went numb. As devastating as it was to lose someone so close to me, his death brought out a new meaning in life for me. I began to realize that life is too short to spend time doing things that I simply do not enjoy. It may not be feasible to just up and quit a job, or end a long term relationship, or divorce your family; however you can take steps to not allow those relationships or commitments to rob you of your joy in life. Joy is a precious commodity. If you find yourself in any situation that is robbing you of the essential joys of life, ask yourself, is it worth trading your joy for?

STEP 2

Stop being afraid of solitude

Solitude is not alone

– Laura Helgoe

You may not believe this, because you think that you only come to your amazing realizations and conclusions when surrounded by others, but some of life's greatest lessons are learned while you are alone. This is because you finally have a chance to look deep inside yourself and allow your true passions and desires to fully express themselves. When you are too inundated with everyone else's opinions of how you should be, what you should do, or where you should go, how are you to know your own desires?

Meditation and solitude allow you a chance to focus on you, and take into account what everyone else has said without them watching and waiting for you to choose a path. It is hard to unplug from society for a few minutes a day, but it is absolutely necessary.

You don't have to be alone for hours or days at a time, but giving yourself a set amount of alone time regularly will bring inner peace and focus to your life you never knew was possible. In the moments when you do find yourself alone, no matter the amount of time, reflect on who you are and what you want out of this life. If you don't take time to listen to yourself, how can you expect anyone else to?

STEP 3

Stop deferring your dreams

Hope deferred makes the heart sick, but when dreams come true, there is life and joy.

– Proverbs 13:12

Do you find yourself making plans to do the next thing when this thing is accomplished? Many people want to make a change in their lives; however the change is often deferred. Take dieting, for instance, why would you wait until tomorrow? Many people dream that "someday" this will happen or that will begin, or they will be happy, "someday." Unfortunately, those people are the ones who learn that "someday" never comes. It is important to learn and understand that life is for living today. Take advantage of your opportunities as and when they arise, not when you get your degree, or get married, or lose 50 lbs.

As the old saying goes, "Why put off until tomorrow, what you could get done today." Dreaming of "someday" is another form of procrastination. Whether it is fear, finances, health, or opposing friends or family holding you back—you need to decide what is more important: happiness or familiarity.

STEP 4

Stop being afraid of rejection

Rejection is God's way of saying wrong direction.

– Unknown

I t happens to the best of us. If it doesn't come your way at some point in life, you are doing something wrong. No matter where the rejection comes from, it is human nature to be hurt over it. The plan for your future is bigger than who you are dating, or who will not date you. If he/she does not want you, now or ever, trust me, this could be the biggest blessing in disguise you have ever received. Man's rejection is God's protection.

If you don't get the job, if he doesn't want to date you, if you aren't invited to the party, there's a reason. Instead of being mad, sad, or angry; be happy about it.

"Happy? How can I be happy when I've been rejected?" You can be happy because God protected you from a situation that was not good for you in some way. Rejection isn't fun, but it isn't fatal either. Trust that something better is on the horizon and that life may not be all you want in this very moment, but being rejected does not define who you are.

STEP 5

Stop being afraid to love just because you are afraid you will lose

There is no fear in love. But perfect love drives out fear, because fear has to do with punishment. The one who fears is not made perfect in love.

– I John 4:18

It happens, trust me. Life has its ups and downs in every facet, but a life that has never loved really has not lived at all. Love is universal. Whether it is romantic love shared with a life partner or a love between family and friends, you need to let people in and allow them to love you while you love them in return. Love fills our soul, inspires our creativity, heals our emotional wounds, and propels us further forward in life. No one is perfect, and relationships do not always last like they do in the love stories, but that doesn't mean the good times weren't good.

You have to keep going even after heartbreak. Not only do you lose the opportunity to love and be happy if you wallow in past heartaches, but you also harm those around you who love you and who want to be loved. Accept the fact that no one is perfect, and everyone is in need of a helping hand sometimes, and love them. The love you receive in return will help heal any past heartache, even without you knowing it.

STEP 6

Stop making excuses for the bad decisions you make

Stop making excuses and start making changes.

– Habeeb Akande

Our parents and our environment only have so much control over us, and you have to understand that what you choose to do with that upbringing is on you. Everyone has challenges, and everyone has to learn how deal with them. If you chose to make a bad decision, it was your choice, therefore you have no one to blame except yourself. Stop making excuses for the bad decisions. If you choose to lie, cheat, steal, and manipulate other people, stop saying it is because of what you were exposed to as a child. That is displaced blame. It is time to heal and time for you to make better choices. Own up to it and change your ways. You will feel better about yourself when you stop making excuses, and eventually you will stop making those bad decisions.

STEP 7

Stop comparing yourself to others

But let each one test his own work, and then his reason to boast will be in himself alone and not in his neighbor.

– Galatians 6:4

Everyone cannot be judged on the same standards. You are your own person and there will never be anyone quite like you. Comparing yourself to others is not only misleading, but it's incredibly damaging. There is power in setting your own benchmarks and striving to accomplish goals that satisfy who you are.

Strive to reach and exceed your own potential. When you begin to trust yourself and guide yourself based on your talents and desires, you will begin to realize that comparing yourself to others is a futile exercise. Comparing yourself to others will only set you on a perpetual cycle of exhausting highs and lows.

STEP 8

Consider the source of your advice

For the time is coming when people will not endure sound teaching, but having itching ears they will accumulate for themselves teachers to suit their own passions.

– 2 Timothy 4:3

It is time to stop relying on friends and family to give you advice for your life decisions, when often times their lives are out of whack. It's one thing if Bill Gates is offering you some financial advice. However, on the contrary, when your sister who borrows money from you every week gives you financial advice, you should consider the source. You have to consider the source, and take each piece of advice with a grain of salt. People have lots of opinions, and since they are free, there is no problem in sharing them with the rest of the world.

However, many people offer a ton of advice, and it appears they are often unable to take their own advice. This is not to say to just brush off all advice, but take it in stride and only use the pieces that fit into your life. When something someone said to you clicks, you will know. It will resonate and stick with you, sort of like an 'aha' moment. Go into every decision with an open mind and a clear heart, but keep in mind someone that has the same struggles as you, and has not overcome the struggles, just may not be the best source to take advice.

STEP 9

Stop wearing mask to fit in

Those who follow the crowd usually get lost in it.

– Rick Warren

Unless you are going to a masquerade party, or dressing up for Halloween, there is no reason for you to hide who you are behind a mask. So often in life we wear a mask to fit in at work, in social settings, and even within our own families. We do this so we are more comfortable, or to make others feel more comfortable around us. One of the great things about humans is that we all share similarities and differences. Being able to share those differences makes us unique and interesting. When you compromise yourself so that others will accept you, everyone is negatively affected. You limit your potential and those around you are given a façade.

If you are in an environment or situation where you do not feel as though you can be your authentic self, this will impact the relationship or situation. It is okay to march to your own beat, and enjoy the music while doing so. That's part of being human, and it's something to embrace. Once you do, your growth potential is limitless and the ability to achieve gets stronger and stronger.

STEP 10

Stop living inside the box

"There is no man living who isn't capable of doing more than he thinks he can do."

– Henry Ford

There once was a group of people who thought the world was flat. Then, one day after discussing and researching, they stepped out of the box and realized that the round earth needed to be discovered. Stop living in your box. It is time to be spontaneous, live, laugh and love. Do it NOW.

You want to live your best life now, before it's too late and the opportunities stop coming. It is not up to you to hold down the world, it is up to you to enjoy yourself and leave the world a better place than how you found it. No one is able to accomplish anything by staying in a box, and hiding from adversity. Spontaneity can be scary, but it can lead to some of the most rewarding opportunities you have ever imagined.

If you don't try something new, you will never know

if it will work. Without the ability to learn and grow, you will eventually get stuck in the past and prevent yourself from moving forward with your life. If you find you are living within the boundaries of a box one you put yourself in or not. It is time to climb out and live life full and complete outside the box.

STEP 11

Stop waiting for approval

Am I now trying to win the approval of human beings, or of God? Or am I trying to please people? If I were still trying to please people, I would not be a servant of Christ.

– Galatians 1:10

You are an adult who is free to make choices and live how you want. You are free to choose your responsibilities and your passions, and it doesn't matter what others think. Unfortunately, most of us never lose that feeling of needing approval. We need approval from our parents, spouses and friends. Your choices are yours; don't allow anyone to tell you differently. If you want to quit your job and start a cookie business, go ahead and do it. Who can stop you from achieving your dreams?

Stop allowing others to negate your desire to succeed. I'm not saying that it is ok to uproot your family without discussing it, or do things that could potentially jeopardize others. It is just time to stop letting others opinions of you rule how and what you choose to do with your life. It is hard to stop wanting the approval of everyone else.

Approval often feels like acceptance, and most people want to feel loved and accepted. It took me many years and hundreds of tears to finally come to a place in my life that I stopped seeking approval of others. We have one shot at this life, live it, follow your dreams and if someone thinks you are crazy for making a mistake, which is completely okay. You have to live and honor your own truths.

STEP 12

Stop being ordinary

The difference between ordinary and extraordinary is that little extra.
– J. Johnson

It is time for you to lead your extraordinary life. You need to let your light shine. We have already discussed the unique abilities that you have and how you have to stop wearing a mask around people. Even if other people do not understand your passions and your light, shine it. Someone else might be inspired to do the same when they see how courageous you are. That voice that you hear inside of you, that will not let you rest, yet keeps telling you are great. That is the truth. It takes absolutely zero extra effort to be ordinary. But to reach your full potential, to be extraordinary, to be all that you know you can be inside is within each of us. It is up to you to shed the layers, climb out the box, and leave your unique stamp on the world.

STEP 13

Stop being judgmental

Judge not, and you will not be judged; condemn not, and you will not be condemned; forgive, and you will be forgive

– Luke 6:37

I am not saying this to clean up the world that is full of hatred. I am not concerned about anyone but you right now. When you judge someone else, it really says more about you than the person whom you have the problem with. When a part of who you are is unsatisfied, it will try to find relief by expressing judgment on someone else's choices. Good or bad, they are not your choices. It is really a deep and hidden form of self-depreciation.

We all have opinions and we all have the right to voice them. However, if the situation doesn't involve you, and it wasn't your choice to make, why judge it?

We already learned that we should stop allowing others opinions rule our lives, so don't try to rule others with your own judgments.

STEP 14

Stop being afraid to live

I know the plans I have for you,' says the Lord. 'They are plans for good and not for disaster, to give you a future and hope.

– Jeremiah 29:11

Being afraid can rob you of your time and happiness without giving you anything but anxiety and stress. Most of the time, the things we are afraid of are not real. We have all heard that FEAR stands for – False Expectations Appearing Real. Not a real object, person, or situation, but something we simply thought might be real.

Often times we are so afraid of the unknown that we do nothing at all to move our life forward. After I lost my love in 2009, so much fear set in, I was afraid to live. I became stuck not only in my grief, but in my fears too. Being afraid to live kept me in a constant state of denial and confusion. My outlook was always negative and dark. Once I began to slowly realize that FEAR was robbing me of living, I slowly began to recognize when I was fretting over the unknown or when my fears were valid. 99% of the time, they were not real fears and life began to seem brighter and happier when I stopped being afraid to live.

STEP 15

Stop giving up too soon

And let us not grow weary of doing good, for in due season we will reap, if we do not give up.

– Galatians 6:9

So close and yet so far! Does this ever feel like you? You are teetering on the edge of success, this close to making it work, but you're too tired to go on so you instead give up. Then it happens, and the moment you were waiting for comes through, only you weren't there to see it because you gave up.

We are an impatient species. I remember being a child and not understanding why it took so long for things to happen, or dates to come around. If I wanted Christmas to come, it seemed as though it took absolutely forever before it actually happened. Now, time goes by faster, but that doesn't make me any less impatient when I'm waiting for something. However, I've learned that being impatient and giving up too soon has caused me to suffer from many unhappy situations both at work and in my personal life.

Obstacles are going to come along, reaching the goals we set, or living the life we wish for is going to slow down at times. If everyone gave up or quit because of the obstacle in front of them, nothing would get accomplished. Don't give up on your goals because of obstacles, just keep striving forward. It is very common that we give up moments before the breakthrough. Patience and courage are two of the most understated and underutilized characteristics we possess. Tap into your patience and courage and watch your goals and dreams manifest in due course.

STEP 16

Stop procrastinating

Procrastination is the thief of time.

– Edward Young

Procrastinator's of the world unite

– Tomorrow!

I've been there, we all have. Sometimes it just seems easier to keep pushing back a task and hoping that the time to start it never comes around. Unfortunately, it usually does, and then I'm rushing around stressed out trying to accomplish something in one day when I've had weeks and weeks to prepare.

Procrastination is merely about putting off important tasks in order to hide from the fear you have of starting that task.

The baby steps of life are the way to approach new projects and situations when you are a procrastinator. Instead of fearing the entire situation, just start with the first step. Once that is over with, and you have some confidence under your belt, take the next step, then the next, and so forth. It becomes easier to handle tasks like this opposed to jumping right in and trying to accomplish the entire project in day one. Don't picture the whole project, picture one small part of it. Once that is finished, picture the next one. This will stop the premature freak-out sessions, and allow you the confidence to get moving again.

There is one surefire way to make sure that you never get something done, wait until Monday to start it. When you want to get something done or want to make a change, starting fresh on Monday will not benefit you whatsoever. This will give you all weekend to make up excuses, forget, and find plenty of other reasons why Monday will never come. Don't put off until tomorrow what you can get done today. You had the idea, the passion, and the willpower today; so do it today!

STEP 17

Stop holding grudges

And whenever you stand praying, forgive, if you have anything against anyone, so that your Father also who is in heaven may forgive you your trespasses.

– Mark 25:11

People make mistakes and accidents happen. You can't stop this part of life, no matter how hard you try. People are going to hurt you, people are going to disappoint. But realize how life will stand still for you if you do not forgive and hold grudges. Holding a grudge will tie you to the past and keep you stuck there feeling miserable.

We are all going to go through life getting hurt and battered emotionally. You have to forgive. It is an essential part of healing and growing. If you want to move on in life, you will forgive those who have given you scars and get over it. I didn't say you have to forget, or accept them again, but you do have to forgive. In your heart, you have to release the anger and stored resentment. You have to allow yourself to move on from the pain and grow over the scar.

Withholding forgiveness doesn't usually affect the offender, but it always effects the offended. You can release the sadness and make room for happiness when you forgive those who have hurt you.

STEP 18

Stop the negative self-talk

Death and life [are] in the power of the tongue: and they that love it shall eat the fruit thereof.

– Proverbs 18:21

This is a tough one because negative self-talk is so prevalent in our society. We are trained by society to hate our bodies, our hair, etc. We are in an environment that values 100% perfection and when something doesn't measure up, there is always a someone standing side court ready to talk negatively. Don't let yourself be a part of this phenomenon.

There is nothing good that can come from putting yourself down. If something needs to be fixed, fix it. Bashing your self-esteem on purpose doesn't sound like a good idea to me, but that is exactly what we do when we say things such as, "I'm not good at that," or "I am too fat…"

Words form our world, and what we say lodges itself down inside of our conscience and start to manifest what was spoken. Our psyche is a very tender part of us, and we often abuse it by pushing ourselves too hard, damaging not only our self-esteem but our drive and focus as well. Success does not come to those that do not believe in themselves.

STEP 19

Stop pushing your fears and negative mindset on other people

You cannot expect to live a positive life if you hang with negative people.

– Joel Osteen

If you do not want others to judge you, you have to stop judging them. It is not your life, even if you think you could live it better. Stop putting your opinions on their plate and asking them to eat it. If they want to take some of your advice, they will do so. If they don't, forcing them into it will not make a stronger relationship. Let people be who they are. They will be happier and so will you. If you turn out to be right, they will feel more comfortable coming to you for emotional support if they don't think they are going to get the "I told you so" lecture from you. Our fears and mindsets are not often things we can easily push aside for ourselves, but they have no place being forced onto others with dreams and aspirations.

Think back to a time when you were so excited

about something, and a fear monger came in and quickly squashed your dreams with their notions of destruction and sadness. When others go blindly into a situation and are bombarded with negativity, they are more than likely going to fail. If you hold your tongue and allow them to proceed, you can be there to support them up, and offer your advice when they need it. Most people won't listen when they are focused on accomplishing something, but when it fails they will ask for direction. Be the person they come to for direction, not the one who pushes them to run blindly without looking back.

STEP 20

Stop limiting your perspective

Those who cannot change their minds cannot change anything.
– George B. Shaw

Picture your future as one with wide open spaces, and lots of room to make all the mistakes and learn all the lessons you can. Don't limit yourself to one way of thinking just because it's the only one you know. Learn to see life from a different perspective, and enjoy it that much more.

The great thing about everyone being different is that you get to see life from a different perspective with every conversation. Your viewpoint is not always the best, nor is it the only one. Therefore, instead of bombarding everyone with your opinion, sit back and enjoy the conversation. Pick up a few ideas from other perspectives and allow your mind to remain open.

If you need to voice concerns or opinions because someone might be in danger, do so in a respectful manner, but do not "Should" people. "You should not do that." These types of statements make people do one of two things, stop and curl into the fetal position, or run away blindly trying to break the chains of command. It's not your life, nor is it your decision. You may be surprised at the outcome when someone approaches a topic in a different way.

STEP 21

Stop fighting the wrong fights

Some of the greatest battles will be fought within the silent chambers of your own soul.

– Ezra T. Benson

It is easy to get into arguments and tiffs when you are close to people. You are opinionated, and so are they, so sparks may fly. Letting them fly at random is dangerous and can burn down a relationship faster than anything else. You have to know when to fight and when to back down. Remember, there are some things are just not worth fighting over.

Growing up, I was told, "Pick your battles." That never really rang true until I got older, because I was tired of fighting every battle that came my way. Some things are just not worth it, either because the outcome will not change or because the person will not change their stance. I realized I didn't need to be the one to try and make them change it. No matter what the issue is, decide whether or not it is a beneficial fight.

If you don't stand to gain happiness, but instead lose friends or family, it's not a good fight. You can express your discontent without causing a fight. Not every single issue deserves your time and attention, so choose wisely. Then, you will reserve your energy for the major battles that come about. Don't squander your "all" before you get to the time and place to use it.

STEP 22

Stop waiting on the wrong people

To everything there is a season, and a time to every purpose under the heaven

– Ecclesiastes 3

S ometimes you have to just let go and agree to live and let live.

As social creatures, we can find it difficult to let go. When you have found someone that you would like something from, whether that's a relationship, romance or collaboration, it's easy to dig your claws in and wait there dangling until they are ready. What happens if they never become ready? What happens when they change their view and you are left without direction?

Don't wait for someone else to fulfill you. You may have not gotten what you wanted from them, but maybe they didn't have it to offer. Sometimes you have to let go and walk your own path. Waiting around for someone to change, or decide they want to be with you only wastes your time, energy, and happiness. Plus, if you just wait around, you may miss opportunities for happiness. Sometimes you have to leave people behind. This may not only be for your benefit, but for theirs as well.

STEP 23

Stop living in the past

To live in the present, you need to act or accept but never stay stuck.

— *John Kuypers*

There is a reason why they call it the past. Mainly, the reason it is behind you is there for a reason. You lived it once and should have learned from it, but that doesn't mean you have to wallow in it. Living in your past makes it impossible to enjoy your present or plan for your future. Plus, if you judge your present off the past, no new experiences will be able to bloom.

Everyone has a past. When you learn to let it go and just keep the lessons learned, you are free to enjoy your present and build your future. Holding onto the past just keeps open a lifeline that is broken on the other end. You don't know it's broken, so you keep holding the string, waiting to pull it whenever you need comfort. Unfortunately, you will pull on it one day to find that it's not attached to anything but you. Leave the past behind you where it belongs and start enjoying today. Your future will thank you.

STEP 24

Stop living for your parent's approval if you are over 25

Train up a child in the way he should go; even when he is old he will not depart from it.

– Proverbs 22:6

P arents love their children at any age. Sometimes the pressure they put on you can be demanding and in order to make you happy, can cause you to stunt your growth. Unfortunately, they can usually tell when you're not happy and it makes them sad. Making sacrifices so that they are happy is not likely to work because they will see through it and will want to suggest other ways to make you happy. Those will also not cut it for you, and the pressure builds. Take a stand, tell them what makes you happy, and stop sacrificing.

They will love you no matter what you do. They will eventually accept you regardless of what choices you make because they are your parents. They may not be happy, and they may not agree, but they don't have to. If they choose to not accept you, that don't mean you are wrong, it means they need to rethink unconditional love. They raised you and taught you their ways. If you choose a different path, they need to have faith that the morals and intelligence they instilled will keep you on the desired path that will make YOU happy. Whether it makes them happy or not, by genetics, they are still your parents.

Living for their approval will keep you in a consistent childhood and it is difficult to make adult decisions when you need their approval. This is as much for your benefit as it is for theirs.

STEP 25

Stop following the crowd

Do not follow the crowd in doing wrong. When you give testimony in a lawsuit, do not pervert justice by siding with the crowd.

– Exodus 23:2

Sheep are great in groups as they love to follow the crowd. People are not meant to be sheep. We are not herd animals, which is why we were given brains and free will. You are an adult and a smart one. Think for yourself and allow your brain to guide you in the decisions you need to make. Don't allow them to come from your neighbor or a sign on the side of the highway. Do not allow the masses to determine your beliefs.

If you are truly a republican or democrat, then great—attend the rally and promote your cause. However, if you have opinions that others don't agree with don't cave and follow the masses because you don't have a friend at your rally. Stand up for your beliefs. Think for yourself. Make your own choices and allow others to make theirs.

And now for a bonus tip!

STEP 26

Stop living without seeing your true essence

Now to him, who is able to do far more abundantly than all that we ask or think, according to the power at work within us.

– Ephesians 3:20

You are a beacon of light and love among the dark seas of life, sharing your gifts and talents with the world. Stop in the morning and look at each day as an opportunity to spread your positivity. Look in the mirror and tell yourself, "I am the greatest. Alexander the Great wishes he could be me."

And then start believing it! Too many people in this world go through life with blinders on about how amazing they are and what gifts they have to offer. No one is better at being you than you are. Enjoy your unique self and put it to good use. Others will benefit from knowing you, and you can inspire countless number of people just by being who you are!

Diminishing this truth about yourself is a detriment to society, as well as to the survival of your soul. You have a beautiful essence and purpose… embrace it.

You have just read the first 26 steps to your "Sweet Spot" – the steps focused on things to stop doing in order to focus and to live life authentically. Next you will find the list of 26 steps you can start doing in order to focus and find your "Sweet Spot". Here is a list of the great steps to get you focused on the positive changes you can make to start living the life you were meant to live.

STEP 27

Learn the value in pleasing God or a higher power above anyone or anything else

You shall love the Lord your God with all your heart and with all your soul and with all your might.

– Deuteronomy 6:5

No matter what religion you are, or faith you belong to, there is a higher power that created this universe. Instead of pleasing others, try pleasing God first. Pray and understand what he has planned for you. Once you understand the path, take the first step. Follow God's plans for your life, otherwise anyone else's plans will fall through.

When you seek to please a human, you work so hard, and finally think you have their requests perfected, and then their pleasure point's change. Humans are finicky people and sometimes change their minds the way the wind blows. Pleasing humans before you focus on pleasing yourself or God is a waste of time. What they liked yesterday that you worked so hard to become has changed by the time you reveal your transformation. God does not change His desires for His children.

There is something to be said about taking the reins out of your own hands and allowing God or your higher power to guide you. You will still have free will to accept or deny his guidance. But keep in mind if you choose his way it will keep you aligned with your goals instead of trying to please everyone around you and sacrificing yourself.

STEP 28

Learn the value in leaving things better than you found them

See, I am doing a new thing! Now it springs up; do you not perceive it? I am making a way in the wilderness and streams in the wasteland.

– Isaiah 43:19

There is a perfect order to most things in life. When order is not respected chaos will settle in. If we would all adopt the philosophy of leaving things better than we found them, the world would be much closer to the paradise we all wish for. Here are some things to do to start living this way, and getting yourself in the habit of leaving things better:

- Pick up trash
- Plant trees
- Conserve water
- Smile
- Lend a helping hand
- Hold doors open
- Give random gifts
- Send thank you notes

- Teach a child to laugh
- Help an animal in need

Whatever the case may be, always strive to leave a trail of happiness behind you when you go. There may not have been a path when you set out, but the trail you left behind you inspired others to follow. Your work here is done!

STEP 29

Learn to invest in your mind, body, and soul.

If you nurture your mind, body, and spirit, your time will expand. You will gain a new perspective that will allow you to accomplish much more.

— *Brian Koslow*

You are a being comprised of mind, body and soul. You can't take care of one without needing to help the others. The three works together to make you who you are. When you get busy and bogged down, they all suffer in their own way. In order to achieve your true potential, it is important to take the time to relax and recharge your batteries. You have to take time for yourself without distractions.

Turn off the electronics and go for a walk. Read a book. Pray or meditate. Do yoga, exercise, etc. Taking time to regenerate your mind as well as your body will allow your soul to succeed in its purpose.

We get bogged down and become the type who can only relax when surfing the internet, or watching a show. It helps turn off our brains from our thoughts and focus on something else. The best way to relax to regenerate your mind, body, and soul is to take a sabbatical. This could be something as simple as time each day to go within in alone time, in the shower, or bath, or just moments before you wake up or go to sleep in day. Take time to just turn the world off and spend one on one time with yourself nourishing your mind, body and soul.

STEP 30

Learn the value in satisfying the people that depend on you daily

As each has received a gift, use it to serve one another, as good stewards of God's varied grace.

– 1Peter 4:10

You are an amazing human being who was put on this Earth to better not only yourself, but to better the other humans put in your path. Those people deserve the best that you have to offer to them.

These people may be your children, spouse, parents or friends. For anyone who depends on you, learn to value of taking care of their needs. Please know that I am not telling you to become a slave or a pushover. However, there is a great satisfaction in knowing that those who depend on you for moral, emotional, physical, or even financial support are satisfied and their needs are being met.

Learn the value in pleasing those that need you so that when they are able, they can use your example to do the same for those that depend on them.

STEP 31

Learn the value in honoring your temple

Or do you not know that your body is a temple of the Holy Spirit within you, whom you have from God? You are not your own, for you were bought with a price. So glorify God in your body.

– 1 Corinthians 6:19-20

God gave you a temple to live in. It is your own personal temple to honor and cherish. This temple is your body. This body is not regenerated when you mess it up. In other words, you don't get second chances. You are given one temple and what you do with it directly effects how long you have it.

Taking care of our bodies has been labeled a luxury or chore. It is neither. While our bodies need massages and healthy foods to keep it running smoothly, they are often deemed as luxuries we should not afford. Eating organically and joining a gym will allow you to better yourself in order to live longer and happier.

Many people, including myself, will spend money making sure our homes or vehicles are well maintained, but we will not spend $30.00 on a 30 day supply of vitamins. Take some time to account for the things you spend your money on each month and ask yourself, what fraction of that goes towards keeping your temple honored. Start investing in your temple and the reward will be far greater than owning the hottest new technology product that will be outdated in 6-12 months.

STEP 32

Learn the value in the quiet

Keep your tongue from evil and your lips from speaking deceit.
— Psalms 34:13

We have talked about recharging your batteries, and making time for yourself. An understated point is to spend time in quiet. It is very important in this day and age to spend at least a small portion of each day unplugged. You need to turn off the noise from the outside world.

In addition to spending time quietly each day, it is also an enhancement to your life to practice not always speaking to be heard, or to validate points of view. Some times less is more. Taking time to just actively listen and not offer any type of feedback will help develop your ability to listen without judging, or placing your point of view in another person's life. Practice the art of quietness and watch how quickly peace will pour into your life.

STEP 33

Learn the value in picking yourself up

I can do all things through him who strengthens me.
– Philippians 4:13

As you know, there will be times in your life that do not go as planned. Being strong and mature means that you will know how to pick yourself up and try again. You have to emotionally climb back up the ladder. When you are flying high and life is great, you never prepare for the fall. Then someone says something, or does something, and you fall off the top rung. The value of picking yourself back up and getting over that disappointment will help you tremendously. You will learn that failing isn't the end. You will learn that you can get back to where you were and begin to succeed again, even if you falter.

When you hit a brick wall, teach yourself to climb over the wall and continue on your journey. This will train you to be an over-comer and this allows for success. When you fall and don't get back up, how do you expect to grow or succeed?

STEP 34

Learn the value in saying no

Being unable to say no can make you exhausted, stressed and irritable.
– Auliq Ice

You are a giving person. You are a talented person. Because of this, people want you to do lots of things and you just can't say no. However, then you get overextended, and start to slack because of your busy schedule. This is when everyone suffers.

Stop taking on too many commitments, and just say no. You are allowed to politely decline. It doesn't mean you don't want to help the person, it just means you are busy in other areas, and taking on their commitments will mean that it won't be done to the best of your ability. Over-committing can lead to stress to yourself and resentment from others.

You need to make a decision about how much you can handle and then say no after that. If you can only commit to 3 engagements a month, then you must promise yourself to decline any further invitations until a spot opens up on your calendar. It can be difficult to do because you think saying no is rejecting someone. Being honest with people about how in order to function at full capacity you have to be diligent with your time, this will let people know that you are honest, and it will keep your life in order and not so chaotic.

You don't want to over extend yourself. Stress, fatigue, and resentment lead to sickness and sadness. These are not positive emotions and you will not see positive outcomes.

STEP 35

Learn the value of saying yes

Yes, when you are sharpened with the true information, you will be motivated to make impacts.

– Israelmore Ayivor

There are events and activities in this world that not only benefit you, but will also benefit others. Make time in your schedule for some of these events. Say, "Yes, I will" when someone asks you to volunteer at a charity event. Learn to give back and offer your hand whenever possible. Giving back to the community and world is gratifying.

When you do something nice for someone, they are not the only one who will leave smiling. You smile, and so do those who watched the act. Learn how to say yes to help other people, even if is just what you perceive to be a small gesture. The smallest gesture can be the biggest change in someone's life. All you had to do was say: "Yes!" Though, when saying yes to others, remember to not overcommit.

STEP 36

Learn the value of closure

Nothing changes until people decide to do the things they must, in order to bring about peace.

– Shannon Alder

There are events that come and those that go. We have often heard that when a door closes in life, another one opens. This holds truth in the fact the opportunity is there and you just have to look for it. However, if you keep thinking about the door that closed, you will be stuck in the past. You may have really wanted to go through that door, but it didn't happen and this may have hurt. However, begging, pleading, crying and banging down the door aren't going to change it.

You need to grasp the idea of closing the door and accepting the change. Staying in the past and holding onto the idea that something different would have, could have, should have happened is not healthy. This will not help you go forward in your search for happiness. Learn how to walk away from the things that no longer serve you, or the things that no longer bring value to your life. This will give you closure in all facets of your life. You will be able to move on and enjoy the future when you aren't tied to what could have been behind the door.

Everything happens for a reason. Once you grasp that, you'll understand the reason is probably more about protecting you and not rejecting you.

STEP 37

Learn the value in defining your happiness

Rejoice in the Lord always; again I will say, Rejoice.

– Philippians 4:4

Learning how to live a life that fits you means that you are going to have to know what makes you happy. You need to decide and learn what it will take to make you happy and strive to make it a reality. The things that make you happy do not have to be extravagant or exuberant. It could be something simple that makes you smile, cry tears of joy or warm your heart. It could be a day in the park with family, reading a book with a cup of tea, or cuddling with your children while watching their favorite movie. Define your happiness, so that you know how to recognize it when it comes around.

Learn what it means to you to be happy and spend time developing a pattern of happy habits. Define them so you do not wake up one day full of regrets because you allowed others or the world define what makes you happy.

STEP 38

Learn the value in appreciating the very small things

Give thanks in all circumstances; for this is the will of God in Christ Jesus for you.

– 1 Thessalonians 5:18

Frequently in life we are waiting on the next big event such as birthdays, showers or weddings. We tend to show a greater appreciation for these monumental events, while overlooking or neglecting the smaller things in life. Today, take some time to reflect on the things that may be neglected. Recognize and appreciate them. Day-by-day I am learning to appreciate the smile from a stranger on a busy day, laughter in a crowded room, an umbrella to shelter from the rain and raindrops on a hot day. Learn the value in appreciating the small things. My motto is: don't sweat the small stuff, appreciate it.

STEP 39

Learn the value in friendship

True friendship is like sound health; the value of it is seldom known until it is lost.

– Charles C. Colton

The support you can get from having friends around is not a feeling you can get from anything else. Everyone needs someone to build their confidence when they've had heartbreak or a letdown. Friends build us up, and push us forward. Having friends to support the many difference facets of life is essential. Imagine your life without your friends and you will imagine a life less than happy. It is important to know what value your friends bring to your life and build your relationship around that value system.

Whether they are lifelong friends who get together every Friday night, or friends you only see once a year but catch up like no days have passed, friendships bring us spice and happiness to our lives that cannot be duplicated. Who else will correctly tell you when you are wrong, messed up and making the wrong decision without sugar coating it? Our friends know us, and it is important to know the value in their support.

STEP 40

Learn the value of being silly

Anyone can be passionate, but it takes real lovers to be silly.

— Rose Franken

There are many things in this world that need seriousness to be completed. There is a time and a place for every emotion, and sometimes we forget to let go and allow the silly emotion to have its time. Seriousness can be necessary, but it can also be boring and draining. It is important to take the time out of your day to be silly and enjoy not having a care in the world. Be silly with your friends, your kids, your spouse, your family. Be silly with yourself and dance in your car. Living life to serious is dull and boring. Tell jokes and make people laugh. Spread joy wherever you go by allowing yourself to be silly when you can.

Children often allow us an excuse to be silly, but you don't need to be a parent or to be around children to let the silliness flow. Just let go, dance like no one is watching, tickle an adult, sing in public and just be free and silly. You will feel renewed and uninhibited.

STEP 41

Learn the value of being neutral

A soft answer turns away wrath, but a harsh word stirs up anger.

— Proverbs 15:1

Most of us are passionate about many different topics of life. However, in a social setting we need to learn to be neutral in open-ended discussions. The neutral person is often the most opened minded and willing to see both sides of the situation. This means they learn more. They learn about different views, walks of life and solutions to common problems. Keeping an open mind keeps you on your toes and allows you to expand your viewpoint. The person that can only see one point of view knows the least about the topic, and that is blatantly obvious when they voice their opinion.

Being close-minded makes one very susceptible to, what I like to call, "rocking boat" syndrome. When someone rocks the boat, or their way of thinking, a close-minded person doesn't know how to react and may make rash decisions. Having more experience, knowledge and ability to understand different viewpoints allows you to take everyone's ideas into account when you make a decision. An open mind allows you to make the best decisions possible in a situation. Being prepared with knowledge will be your best defense in times of need. Remain neutral in your conversations and you're learning. Hold fast to your beliefs, but don't be afraid to let other ideas make their presence known.

STEP 42

Learn the value in cultural diversity

There is neither Jew nor Greek, there is neither slave nor free, there is no male and female, for you are all one in Christ Jesus.

– Galatians 3:28

Living in a world full of variety is an amazing asset. Being able to connect with those cultures like never before because of technology and travel means that we have limitless potential to learn about the different cultures of the world. Having friends from many different walks of life and different cultures will allow you to learn and gain insight and perspectives from a multitude of people.

Different cultures have different opinions and viewpoints that are deep and exciting. You would benefit greatly from learning about them so that you can take your experience with you through life and grasp the concepts that make the most sense to you. As we grow through life and learn different cultures, we are able to piece together who we want to be and can inspire others to find their true happiness. Some of the richest experiences I have experienced in life have been from other cultures. It is exciting to learn about different people and how life is so different but how we universally share commonalties.

STEP 43

Learn the value in knowing there is always a threshold

For each will have to bear his own load.

– Galatians 6:5

It is a good thing to have a threshold because then you'll know your boundaries and won't cross them. You need to have a threshold when it comes to your comfort zones and your ideas, that way you will only go as far as you are comfortable with. That is good because you can't be persuaded to go beyond your threshold and won't make mistakes that could harm you.

Everyone has a different threshold and keeping it intact is a strong skill. It teaches you to not ask for more than you are willing to give. You will also learn to not expect more than you can deliver. You will know that there are boundaries in all things: work and play. Know your limits and respect those of others. It is not fair to expect others to follow your threshold limits if you are not willing to follow theirs.

Respect is important in every relationship. Respecting boundaries is important to making, keeping and enjoying each person in your life. You can follow the "to each their own" mindset and know that every person has a threshold that makes sense to them.

STEP 44

Learn the value in ownership

On the first day of every week, each of you is to put something aside and store it up, as he may prosper, so that there will be no collecting when I come.

– 1 Corinthians 16:2

In life we are all going to work and dedicate our time and attention to a job or some activity that will provide an income. In life make it a goal to own something for all the effort you put into making a living. It may not be something expansive like a million dollar home, or a beachfront property, but something of value to you: a pair of diamond earrings, a pearl necklace, a house, a car or property. It does not matter what it is or even the value, just make sure it is something you value and can say is yours.

This will give you a lot of passion and excitement for the future if you value ownership, because you will enjoy the process of acquiring and admiring.

STEP 45

Learn the value in leaving a legacy behind

A good man leaves an inheritance to his children's children, but the sinner's wealth is laid up for the righteous.

– Proverbs 13:22

When you leave this world, what will people say about you? What will you be known for? Leave something behind for your family to value. They will remember you and carry on your legacy in a manner you cannot do yourself. If you teach your ways and your passions, you will be able to inspire others to take it on after you are gone and carry forward with your dreams.

This passion could be a business that you built from the ground up and pass on to your surviving family members. It could be a book that you write about your memories and the family. Maybe you are an activist changing the world one protest at a time. Being known this way will help you to pass on your beliefs and values to your future generations and leave the world a better place than when you entered it.

Your family is going to want to keep your memory and your passions going after you are gone from this world. Leaving them something to respect you for and inspire them to be better people themselves is the ultimate goodbye gift. It's about leaving behind a passion, not about having money and leaving behind a fortune. Leave behind you the tips and tricks you picked up along the way, and the good that you did with those knowledge nuggets in order for the legacy to carry on.

STEP 46

Learn the value of keeping your word

Sanctify them in the truth; your word is truth.

– John 17:17

When you say you are going to do something, do it. In the old days, a handshake meant that you would stick to your word. Saying, "I'll do it," meant that someone could count on you. Nowadays, we need a signed contract between family members to rent out a house. We have lost some of our dignity with the loss of our word. Help bring that value back, and be someone who can be relied on to keep their word.

Be who you say you are and do what you say you will do. Your word binds you to your character. A good character is someone who knows what they want, does what they think is right and helps others when they notice the need. If you want to be known as a good person with good moral character who can be relied upon in the future, stick to your word. Once you break trust with someone, it is very difficult to get that bond back. Sometimes, it is impossible. There are people in this world who forgive, but choose to never forget the damage done. Those people may need to read my section on holding grudges –but in any case – If you break a promise to them, they are more than likely going to forgive you yet never speak to you again.

Keeping your word is as important to you as it is to them. It's hard to come back from a time when you disappointed someone by breaking a promise. They will always have it in the back of their mind that you are willing to back out on them. In order to have faith in yourself and allow others to have faith in you as well it is important to always strive to be a person of value.

STEP 47

Learn the value of progression

For this I toil, struggling with all his energy that he powerfully works within me.

– Colossians 1:29

Progression is moving forward in your life. Making progress means that you have had adversity and are moving past it to create a better future—you are progressing. This means you are growing, maturing and changing for the better. If you are not growing you are dying spiritually, emotionally and mentally. Make everyday a day of progress.

Learn how to push past complacency and grow as a person. Grow your mind, evolve your thinking and ideas, and shape your future into what you want it to be. Never give up on trying to find out what will benefit the world the best way possible and how you can help, and continue to progress towards your goals and ambitions.

STEP 48

Learn the value of losing

Failure is not fatal, but failure to change might be.

– John Wooten

Sometimes, it is important to be good at your skills and to kick butt and take names when you play games. Other times, it is merely about the fun of the game and being able to share time with those you care about. Life is not always about winning, just being involved is rewarding enough. And the lessons you can learn by losing are irreplaceable. Winning is nice, do not get me wrong. However, if you push so hard to win that you alienate yourself or others, it is not worth it. When you realize that winning isn't everything, you start to value how you play the game. This means, in life, you start to value the journey not the destination.

Being able to say that you played along and did the best you could is what matters most when the game is over. Sure a trophy would look nice on the wall, but not all aspects of life give a trophy when you are the winner. Sometimes, not coming in first place means that you learn more lessons and can take away more experience than those who did win. There is a value in coming in behind first place, and that is learning to strive harder, focus on your strengths and take the information you learned in losing to push yourself to do better next time.

Don't push yourself to win, push yourself to beat your last record. Progress is different than perfection. Needing to win is about perfection and can lead to much stress and/or heartache, whereas creating progress is always a good option. A healthy dose of competiveness is okay and will keep you on your toes, but sometimes we are fighting so hard to win a title that we do not fully understand what having it will do to our lives. Or what not having it won't do.

Winning isn't everything.

STEP 49

Learn the value opposites

The universe maintained a balance, moving first one way and then the other in a forever equalizing of opposites.

– *Diana Lanham*

Having a sunny day is amazing. Especially if it happens on your day off. You can accomplish a lot outside, around the house, around the town, and even around the lounge chair sipping cocktails. However, that doesn't mean that if it is a rainy day that should deem a different result. Learn the value of rain or shine.

We look forward to sunshine and frown upon the rain. In our lives, we are going to have sunshine and thunderstorm experiences that can leave us invigorated or depleted. Choose to value both and remember, in the plant world it takes both sunshine and rain to grow. One of my favorite songs is Joy and Pain by "Maze". My favorite verse says; Joy and Pain is like Sunshine and Rain. This is such a true statement as both are essential for cultivation and success. We can't not grow without both rain and sun.

STEP 50

Learn the value of living without clutter

And when it comes, it finds the house swept and put in order.

– Luke 11:25

There is a show on American television about people who don't throw things away. They keep everything from used tissue and wrapping paper to old socks and boxes of clothing. Their houses are cluttered and their lives are a mess, both figuratively and literally. When you learn to accept clutter and allow it to pile up in your home or car, you are accepting stress. You are basically asking to take on more stress with each pile you make on the table. Learn the value in taking time to organize your life, your home, and your mind. This will save a lot of time and frustration.

STEP 51

Learn the value in knowing someone
older and wiser.

Let the elders who rule well be considered worthy of double honor, especially those who labor in preaching and teaching.

– 1 Timothy 5:17

You can learn much from generations of knowledge passed on to you. If you are not lucky enough to visit with elderly family members (such as grandparents or aunts and uncles) maybe you can find a nursing home that allows visitors.

There is so much knowledge and wisdom from the older generations as they have lived many years on the Earth. Just sitting and chatting with someone older and wiser can give you a fresh perspective on your life, as well as hope for your future. Sometimes we get too exhausted in our day-to-day life and get stuck in a rut. Talking with someone who has been there and can offer advice is a good way to relieve that pressure without causing harm. Imagine yourself when you are older and wiser—all the lessons you have learned in your lifetime should be passed on to those who could benefit from it.

Much can be gained from all the knowledge and insight the elderly possess. If you don't take them up on their offer to talk, someone else will. Why would you let that knowledge go to waste?

STEP 52

Learn the value in loving and accepting who you are right now

For you were bought with a price. So glorify God in your body.
— 1 Corinthians 6:20

There are so many things you do right and so many people who love you. It would be great if you could value and love yourself just as much. God does not make mistakes. You are not lost just because you have taken some wrong turns in your life. There is more to the story than the first chapter. Be prepared to ask for His assistance and recreate yourself when you need to. He does not mind recreating who we are when necessary, but we have to ask and be willing to listen.

Knowing that God made you the way you are for a reason should be a comforting thought. Everything about you from your skills to your flaws was on purpose. If not for you, for the people that He knew you would impact on a daily basis. Half of the fun in growing up is learning who you are authentically. Look at your life, goals, aspirations and accomplishments. You are perfect right now in this moment. Keep growing and breaking the chains that bind by applying these 52 steps that will help navigate your life from Wandering to Wonderful!

Conclusion

There you have it, 52 ways you can take control and start living the life you were meant to live. The life that fits you perfectly, instead of one you settled into. As I mentioned in the opening, life is too short to let it slip away from you without being as happy and successful as you possibly can.

Study the steps you just read and think about which ones relate to you the most. Go over them once or twice and then decide to make the changes that will benefit your life the most. Life changes are all about the baby steps, so it doesn't require a huge leap of faith to start living your best life today!

Here's a good way to know if you are on the right track-- map your stress levels and see if they decrease once you start living more towards your passions and dreams and less toward the route society had planned for you. You are a unique and lovely individual. Admire that in yourself and let it shine so that others can admire it as well. There is no better feeling in this world than being true to yourself, and inspiring others by your example because they love who you are, not who you pretend to be just to fit in.

This life is about YOU! Are you going to live it your way?

www.ingramcontent.com/pod-product-compliance
Lightning Source LLC
LaVergne TN
LVHW021611080426
835510LV00019B/2516